ACCIDENTAL INVENTIONS

that changed our world

50 True Stories of Mistakes

That Actually Worked and Their Origins

TABLE OF CONTENTS

Table of Contents 4

Introduction 7

CHAPTER 1
ACCIDENTALLY FUN 9

Snow Globe 11

Silly Putty 13

Play-Doh 15

Slinky 17

Glow Stick 19

Frisbee 21

Basketball Hoop and Backboard 23

Fireworks 26

CHAPTER 2
ACCIDENTALLY YUMMY 29

Chocolate Chip Cookies 31

Coca-Cola 33

Potato Chips 35

Popsicles 37

Ice Cream Cones 39

Cheese 41

Donuts 43

The Tea Bag 45

Worcestershire Sauce 47

The Sandwich 49

Licorice 51

Raisins 53

Chewing Gum 55

CHAPTER 3
ACCIDENTALLY LIFESAVING 57

Aspirin 59

Insulin 62

Anesthesia 64

The Pacemaker 66

Penicillin 68

X-Rays 70

Color-Blind Glasses 72

Vaseline 74

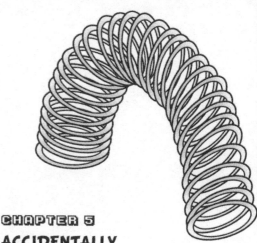

CHAPTER 4
ACCIDENTALLY AROUND THE HOUSE 77

Safety Pins **79**

Velcro **81**

Smoke Detectors **83**

Teflon **85**

Microwave Ovens **87**

Matches **89**

Post-it Notes **91**

Plastic **93**

Paper Towels **95**

CHAPTER 5
ACCIDENTALLY INDUSTRIAL 97

Dynamite **99**

Safety Glasses **101**

Vulcanized Rubber **103**

Smart Dust **105**

Kevlar **107**

Stainless Steel **109**

CHAPTER 6
ACCIDENTALLY ACCIDENTAL 111

Bubble Wrap **113**

Wireless Internet **115**

Mauve **117**

The Telephone **119**

Dry Cleaning **121**

Superglue **123**

Conclusion **125**

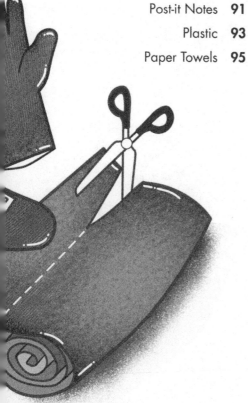

INTRODUCTION

We spend much of our lives benefiting from the strange and ingenious inventions that people have created throughout history. Whether it be as simple as a wheel or as complex as an airplane, we humans are curious creatures and are always looking for ways to improve our lives. Innovation is a wild and interesting thing, but most often of all, it is random.

How and why we get the ideas we do is a completely different story each time and, even when we do get an idea beforehand, its execution doesn't always go according to plan. You might try to come up with a new mattress and end up getting a light bulb instead. This is why, be it a mistake in a process or an 'accident gone right', many human inventions are entirely accidental.

So, read along as we explore all the wondrous things people have invented simply by chance or while shooting for a completely different mark. Accidents happen, and these accidents make for great stories.

This book uses some terms or words that you might not know the meaning of, so in order to make this an easy read, I am going to explain what they mean before we begin.

A "patent" is a legal document that says that you are the only person that can make a certain something and that, legally, you are the person who invented it.

A "eureka moment" is when someone has a sudden and often brilliant idea. The origin of this phrase is from a long story about ancient Greece and bathtubs, which we will not be getting into here (the phrase, not the bathtubs!).

CHAPTER 1
ACCIDENTALLY FUN

Today, toys and games constitute a massive business that makes millions of dollars every year. Entire companies are dedicated to the development of toys and other items for entertainment. Researchers work countless hours in labs coming up with new things to amuse and excite people and artists make hundreds of different models for new dolls or action figures.

However, most of the toys that were developed before some of us were even born were stumbled upon unintentionally or were created accidentally.

Whether it be old items that were repurposed or something serious that took on a fun twist, toy invention still required a great deal of creativity. All of the items in this chapter are things that bring joy, but which were originally intended to have more practical purposes.

SNOW GLOBE

In the late 19th century, some tinkering on the part of Erwin Perzy resulted in the invention of the first-ever snow globe. Perzy was trying to invent a better light source and to make improvements to the very recently invented light bulb.

By day, Erwin Perzy worked as a supplier of medical instruments to local doctors. One of the surgeons he supplied asked him if he could make a light bulb that could provide more and better light than the ones that were currently available. Up for the challenge, Perzy set out to make the best light bulb possible.

His idea for the new light bulb was based on what he had seen shoemakers do. They would take a glass of water and place it near a candle to reflect a section of brighter, more focused light. He believed that submerging the light bulb in water, or some kind of fluid, was the solution to expanding and focusing the light.

So, Perzy tried it out, and he also sprinkled some glitter in the water to make it more reflective. However, the glitter sank too quickly, so he swapped it out for semolina flakes. These did not work either, but the little white flakes reminded Perzy of snow. This was the most basic idea for a snow globe. Perzy then went on to add a miniature diorama or small figurine to the globe. Soon after, he was filing a patent for the first-ever snow globe, or *Schneekugel*.

In the following years, snow globes became increasingly popular among Austrians as both a souvenir and a decoration. They later made their way to America, where a man, called Joseph Garaja, applied for the first American patent and invented something else new; underwater assembly. This meant that snow globes could be filled all the way up with water, making them a lot cheaper and therefore more common.

Even though most snow globes are now made in factories by large machines and are no longer made of pewter and glass, but rather mostly of plastic, there is still a market for handmade, high-quality globes. The original Perzy family still produces thousands of globes every year and has even custom made globes for people such as Barack Obama and Bill Clinton.

Snow globes have mystified people all over the world with their whimsical nature. It's a good thing Perzy never invented that new light bulb.

SiLLY PUTTY

Silly putty really is quite silly. It's a suitable name for a rather strange toy that can both confuse and delight. It's enjoyable to pull between your hands and mold into all sorts of strange shapes and images.

During the Second World War, the American rubber supply was threatened, so the US War Production Board commissioned the General Electric lab in Connecticut to try to come up with a substitute synthetic rubber, which was easy to produce. Engineer, James Wright, who was working there at the time, decided to drop boric acid into silicone oil, and the result was a substance that was stretchier and bouncier than rubber. The substance was an odd mix between a liquid and a solid and shattered when struck with enough sudden force.

As interesting as his invention was, it was not a suitable replacement for rubber. The government named it "nutty putty" and said that there was nothing that could be done with it. However, only a few years later, businessman, Peter Hodgson, saw the potential of this "nutty putty", to be a children's toy.

He noticed how nutty putty was enjoyed at parties and he went on to market it as a children's toy in colorful eggs that released around Easter-time. Even though Peter Hodgson was in a large amount of debt at the time, he chose to take out a loan to buy larger quantities of nutty putty. Borrowing money might have seemed like a very bad idea, but it turned out to be the best decision he ever made. Because of his science-project-turned-toy, Hodgson died a millionaire.

Silly Putty soon became one of the most popular toys, thanks in part to its being featured in a *New Yorker* article, "Talk of the Town." Although the putty was originally only marketed as a toy, some users have discovered many very useful functions for it. One of these is that it can function as a temporary adhesive, which was very useful on the Apollo 8 spacecraft, where astronauts used it to hold down their tools in the zero gravity atmosphere.

PLAY-DOH

Play-Doh is such a well-known substance that many of us can recall exactly how it smells just by thinking about it—maybe some of us can even recall how it tastes too.

Play-Doh's history started with coal. Now, that may sound rather dull, but before the age of electric heating and gas heaters, homes were kept warm with coal burners. These burners left a sticky, black residue on wallpaper that could not be cleaned off with any of the products that were available at the time. Most cleaning agents just smudged the residue and make the staining worse, because of the material that wallpaper was made from.

The Kroger grocery store in Cincinnati found the solution to this problem in Kutol. Kutol was a pliable, off-white, putty-like material that could pull the residue off the walls without damaging the wallpaper, and—for a while—it was a highly sought-after product. However, with the invention of vinyl wallpaper and cleaner gas burners, the product was no longer necessary and sales began to decline massively.

Eventually, Kay Zufall, a nursery school teacher was the person who saved Kutol's sales. She had read an article about how children were using wall putty for art projects and saw the potential for the putty to be a toy. She was the sister-in-law of Joseph McVicker, whose uncle was Noah McVicker, and both men worked at Kutol. Kay convinced them to start marketing and selling the putty as a toy.

The McVikers set up a company called the Rainbow Crafts Company, which was designed purely to manufacture Play-Doh and to make children's toys.

Originally, Play-Doh could only be bought in its original off-white color, but very soon the Rainbow Crafts Company began selling it in yellow, blue and red. Those colors became iconic of Play-Doh. You can get it in even more colors now, but yellow, blue and red will always be the most well-known ones.

The exact recipe for Play-Doh is still a trade secret, even though there are hundreds of recipes on the internet, for people to make it at home. Hasbro, the company that now owns and makes the original Play-Doh, has said that the main ingredients are water, salt, and flour, but the ratio of these ingredients is still unknown.

Play-Doh is a staple in many children's lives and is a great example of how creativity can bring fortune.

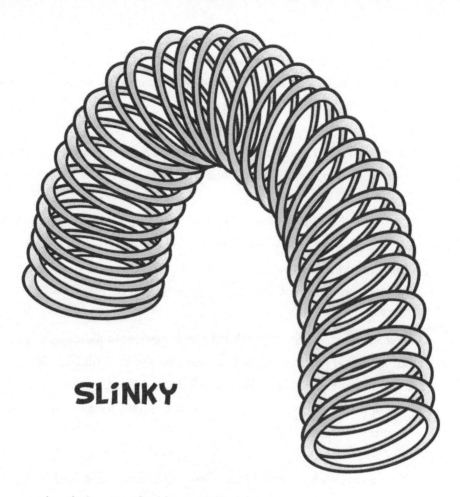

SLINKY

Everyone has been mystified by a Slinky at some
time or another (and quite a few of us have tangled them beyond
repair as well). Slinkies have a rather humble origin.

The Slinky was invented by Richard James, at a time when he was
working in a shipyard in Philadelphia, as a naval engineer. James
was attempting to perfect the tension in the springs used in sensitive
instruments on US ships, so that they would be protected from the
elements of the sea and the navy's daily activities.

James had already made many different springs, with different
tensions and dimensions. They all sat on his desk at work and, as
fate would have it, one of them had the perfect specifications for

a toy. This particular spring did not bounce or flop around as the other springs he had been working on did. Instead, when under the influence of gravity, it slithered.

He later said that he watched it "walk down from its spot" and the idea struck him; what if there was a toy that walked?

James then had his brilliant idea and, with the help of his wife, Betty, he created one of the greatest toys of all time. Betty also saw the potential of the toy and was the person who gave it its name: Slinky. Slinky means graceful or sinuous in movement.

Over the next few years, Richard James perfected the design, so that it had no tension or compression and could 'walk' flawlessly down stairs. He released the toy in 1945, and although sales were slow at first, it became a massive hit after it was featured in Gimbels department store.

The toy was such a big hit that over 100 million were sold in the first two years. Today, many consider it a must-have toy. Everyone has had a Slinky at some point in their life. Today's Slinky is quite different from its original metal form. Most of the ones that you can find on the shelves of today's shops are made of flexible plastic, but they are still just as enjoyable and interesting. And they can certainly walk like no other toy.

GLOW STiCK

Glow sticks are a source of curious awe. The satisfying snap that then releases the bright and exciting neon glow is fun for anyone. Whether you wear them as jewelry or use them to fight intergalactic battles, glow sticks are a great source of light and entertainment.

The invention of these sticks is attributed to Edwin A. Chandross. He was the first person to invent the chemical compound that makes glow sticks glow, and he did so by chance.

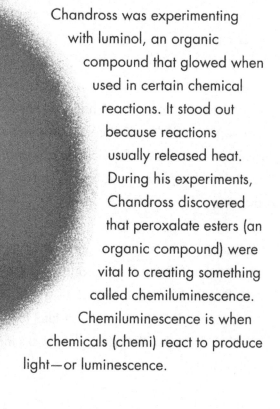

Chandross was experimenting with luminol, an organic compound that glowed when used in certain chemical reactions. It stood out because reactions usually released heat. During his experiments, Chandross discovered that peroxalate esters (an organic compound) were vital to creating something called chemiluminescence. Chemiluminescence is when chemicals (chemi) react to produce light—or luminescence.

Chandross continued to fiddle with and adjust the chemistry, until he found the winning combination: hydrogen peroxide mixed with oxalyl chloride and dye. This compound produced just 0.1% of the light that modern glow sticks do (Sarah, 2015).

Chandross did not know it at the time, but his discovery was monumental for chemistry, and all of the further advancements in chemiluminescence chemistry that followed were thanks to his discovery.

Although he made the discovery, Chandross did not invent the glow stick that was eventually patented. The first glow stick was perfected by Michael M. Rauhut of American Cyanamid. His team improved on Chandross's invention by creating a new chemical that provided a better glow. This substance was trademarked Cyalume and was mostly used for military operations and was not available, at first, for public use.

The sticks later hit the public market and become a fan favorite at parties and concerts. What is interesting is that Chandross, the original mind behind chemiluminescence, had no idea that his invention was so popular. He only found out, when a reporter contacted him, wanting to ask him about his wonderful scientific discovery.

"Is that so?" Chandross laughed when the reporter told him and then he said, "Maybe my granddaughter will think I am cool now" (Gaston, 2013). Well, even if his granddaughter doesn't think he's cool, many other people are grateful for his awesome and forward-thinking discovery. Besides, glow sticks made up for any of his past 'uncoolness'.

FRISBEE

We all know that picturesque scene in a park from a movie; sweet, soft music plays as a Frisbee comes into view chased by a pretty dog who jumps effortlessly to catch it.

Frisbees are a great way to spend time outdoors and to play games that are less strenuous than soccer or tag, for example. However, the idea for this toy actually came from pies.

What do you do with an empty pie tin? It's a lightweight disk that could be used for just about anything, and to the students at Yale University, it was a toy. There was a pie company, Frisbie Pies, situated near Yale's campus, and their pies were a popular study snack among the students. Students often threw the empty tins to their friends on campus, while yelling "Frisbie!" It was their playfulness that sparked the invention of the toy.

Warren Franscioni and Walter Frederick Morrison partnered, to develop a plastic version of the pie disks that were flying around the Yale campus. They were inspired by the students, but their version flew further and faster than its pie-tin inspiration. They named their invention "flying saucers." They hoped this name would capitalize on the space craze that America was going through as well as the fascination surrounding unidentified flying objects (UFOs).

The invention was later sold to the Wham-O toy company, after Morrison and Franscioni split, and it was renamed the "Pluto Platter" to follow along with the space theme and to help to market the product.

In 1958, Wham-O changed the name of the toy to "Frisbee," purposely misspelling the name of the pie company that had started it all. The design was changed slightly and ridges were added to make it fly better, and then this new design was patented by Ed Headrick.

Wham-O managed to sell over 100 million of the toys by 1977 by marketing Frisbee as a new and exciting sport. The original sport of Frisbee soon gained a brother and sister, ultimate Frisbee and Frisbee golf, which only made the toy even more popular in America.

Today there are over 60 manufacturers of the toy, most of which are made out of plastic. Whether it be pie tins or flying saucers, Frisbees have become a well-loved toy and a great game to play at a picnic.

BASKETBALL HOOP
AND BACKBOARD

Unlike most sports, which develop over time, basketball was invented entirely from scratch. It didn't slowly evolve from one sport, but instead, it came into being relatively quickly.

Today, National Basketball Association (NBA) games are some of the most-watched sporting events in the world, and finals often pull in over 5.8 million viewers (Adgate, 2022).

When James Naismith invented basketball, he was not trying to come up with a new sport and had no idea how popular it would become. Rather, he was trying to keep his students at the International YMCA Training School entertained. It was winter, which meant that the students could not play games outside because of the cold.

His aim was to come up with a game that kept them interested, but which did not result in any injuries; therefore, it couldn't be rough. The game had to be able to be played indoors and he wanted it to be simple, without many rules.

The first basketball "hoop" was a broken peach basket. The thing was, Naismith did not want a hoop—he actually approached the janitor for boxes that he could use as goals but was given two baskets instead. Making do with what he had, he fastened them to the

railings of the gymnasium's balcony. This is why the basketball hoop is 10 feet high—that was how high the railings were.

Funnily enough, the first game ended with the students fighting each other. Naismith quickly put an end to the game, thinking it would be the first and last time that they played it. But the students kept nagging him to play again, so Naismith had to put rules in place so that they could play safely.

Later on, a net was added to the hoop to help the ball fall through the hoop; it wasn't exactly accidental, but it is still an important part of play. The net imitated the bottom part of the original basket from which it came.

The backboard was never designed to assist play; rather, it was built to help protect the spectators sitting in the stands behind the hoops. The balls could go flying over the rail and could easily injure people watching the game, so the gyms added backboards to protect the spectators.

Today, backboards are no longer used for this purpose. Instead, they assist players in shooting at their opponent's hoop and defending their own. This development was completely accidental and came from the players' realizing that they could use the backboard to assist their shots. There are now all sorts of rules concerning the backboard and how it can be used.

Basketball is one of the fastest-growing sports of all time and has swept across America and the world. And to think it all started with a teacher trying to keep his bored students entertained.

FiREWORKS

Fireworks—also called firecrackers—were invented in the quest for immortality. At least, that's how one story goes. It's a little unclear exactly, how the first firecrackers came about, but what *is* clear is that it happened around 200 B.C.E., and that they were invented in China.

One story goes that a Chinese alchemist mixed sulfur, charcoal, and potassium nitrate in the hope that this would grant him eternal life. When the powder was set on fire, it exploded and became the first-ever gunpowder. Later, they poured this powder into bamboo sticks and ignited them to make the world's first fireworks.

The early fireworks were used to celebrate important events and to ward off evil spirits, but there wasn't much to them other than the noise of an explosion and maybe some bits of flying debris. They also did not shoot up into the air and were simply tossed into a fire rather than sent flying.

In the years that followed, the Chinese modified the use of this powder for military uses. The first rocket cannons were invented, and they gave way to the first-ever aerial fireworks.

The technology quickly made its way to the West, after European and Arabian diplomats and missionaries visited China. Like their Chinese counterparts, the European engineers used the technology to improve

their military tools, and they also continued the development of fireworks into a wondrous form of entertainment.

Fireworks in the 1600s were not that much different from their origins, but they were now airborne and gave a beautiful display of orange sparks. They were used for military victories, weddings, and royal celebrations, although it was very dangerous work operating them. The shows were run by "fire-masters," and the actual firework cannons were operated by "green men," who got their name from the leaves they wore to protect themselves from the sparks. The green men often told jokes to the crowd while they prepared the fireworks. Despite their comedy, the profession was highly dangerous and many green men were killed or injured on the job.

It was only in the 1830s that fireworks became more colorful, thanks to Italian engineers. They mixed the original gunpowder compound with various metals to give the sparks interesting and exciting colors.

Fireworks today are complex, both in their colors and the shapes they form in the sky. They may not grant you immortality, but they do make you feel alive as you watch them boom in the sky.

CHAPTER 2
ACCIDENTALLY YUMMY

If there is one thing people are good at, it is creating delicious food—not to mention eating it! Food is a very important part of our culture and how we connect with other humans. Many of our most important interactions occur over a meal, and food is even said to help deepen and improve relationships.

Sometimes, we create things in the kitchen that we never intended to. More often than not, these creations are only meant for one thing; the garbage. But, every once in a while, a chef or even an ordinary person will stumble across something that is both clever and delicious.

This chapter will explore some yummy things that make your taste buds dance, but which were discovered without even trying or simply through a twist of fate.

CHOCOLATE CHIP COOKIES

Chocolate chip cookies are a great bringer of joy to many of us. From the perfect movie scene of a kid coming home after a rough day of school to find their mom waiting with freshly baked chocolate chip cookies to a quick, easy, and delicious pick-me-up, chocolate chip cookies are a staple in everyone's lives.

This delicious treat was invented by Ruth Wakefield, and she did it by chance, after an afternoon baking session did not go as planned. Ruth was the owner of Toll House—a bed-and-breakfast—and she worked hard to provide delicious food and treats for all of her guests. Her go-to sweet treat was her Butter Drop Do cookies, and while she was making these particular cookies, one afternoon, she accidentally invented chocolate chip cookies.

Butter Drop Do cookies require baker's chocolate that melts into the batter while the cookies are baking and leaves behind a beautiful chocolate flavor. That afternoon, Ruth ran into a problem; it seemed that her pantry was not as well-stocked as she had thought, and she discovered that she did not have any baker's chocolate. Ruth did not want to throw away the batter she had already spent her precious time making and so she decided to make do with what she had.

She substituted the baker's chocolate with finely chopped semisweet chocolate, hoping that it would do the trick. However, when she removed the cookies from the oven, she was met with a rather different situation. The "chips" had not melted into the batter as baker's chocolate did, but instead had retained their shape and only softened a little.

Ruth named the cookies Toll House Crunch Cookies. They soon became extremely popular, not only with her guests but also with people all over the world. Soon, people started calling them chocolate chip cookies and began trying to make them at home.

In fact, chocolate chip cookies are so popular in America that one-fourth of all the cookies produced in America are chocolate chips (DiNuzzo, 2019). In England, "cookie" is a term only used for chocolate chip cookies; all other variants are called "biscuits."

It is a wonderful thing that Ruth Wakefield's pantry was missing some key ingredients that day. If this hadn't been the case, we might never have been blessed with chocolate chip cookies, and that would have been a terrible tragedy.

COCA-COLA

There is probably no beverage more famous than Coca-Cola. More than 1.9 billion servings of the drink are consumed every day in 200 countries, according to the company (Coca-Cola, 2020). It's safe to say that Coca-Cola has made its mark on the world.

But, believe it or not, Coca-Cola was never meant to be a beverage to enjoy. Rather, it started out as medicine.

Coca-Cola was invented by Dr. John Pemberton, a pharmacist, who had a long-standing gift for chemistry. After studying pharmacy, he fought in the American Civil War, where he was stabbed in the chest in combat. He recovered from the wound, but was left with a morphine addiction.

Pemberton began researching an opium-free painkiller, so that no one else would have to go through the addiction, which he struggled with, to manage their pain. It was during his experimentation that he created the first version of Coca-Cola. He was working with cola nuts and coca wine, and he found a recipe for cola nut extracts and damiana that, when blended into a syrup, had a new and unique taste.

He began to sell the drink as a cure for headaches, exhaustion, and to help calm the nerves. It was originally called "Pemberton's French Wine Coca" and was said to be a medicine. Pemberton later had to change the recipe, due to public concern about alcohol addiction. The new recipe came from his assistant, who accidentally added the base syrup to carbonated water. The new drink was surprisingly refreshing and presented Pemberton with the perfect alternative to alcohol.

This new concoction was called "Coca-Cola" due to its two main ingredients, "coca" and "cola." However, due to the controversy that Coca-Cola was actually made from cocaine, the company had to say that the name was meaningless alliteration. It was then changed from being categorized as medicine to being a "fountain drink."

Coca-Cola's ingredients remained a secret for nearly 100 years, and even to this day, the exact ratios and recipe are a trade secret. This can clearly be seen by all the alternatives that have popped up over the years that just don't taste the same.

Something quite interesting is that the drink does have medicinal properties and has been shown to treat nausea and stomach blockages. Regardless of whether it is medicine or a cure for thirst on a hot summer's day, Coca-Cola has become a staple in America and across the world. Summer would not be the same without it.

POTATO CHiPS

Potato chips are one of those things that life just wouldn't be the same without. Whether it's watching a movie, chatting at a party, or as snacks on a road trip, potato chips just make most occasions better and they are one of the most popular snacks in America.

Just who was responsible for the invention of potato chips is somewhat unclear, and their created has been attributed to many people. All of the most popular stories come out of Moon's Lake House, a popular restaurant in the vacation spot of Saratoga Springs, New York.

The original story goes that a guest at the restaurant, Cornelius Vanderbilt, ordered fried potatoes with his meal and was disappointed when they were not crunchy enough. He asked for them to be sliced thinner. Slightly annoyed, the restaurant's well-known chef, George Crum, sliced them as thin as he possibly could and then refried them. He was trying to prove to Vanderbilt that the way the chips were originally was better; however, much to Crum's surprise, Vanderbilt loved them and, thus, the potato chip was born.

Another story gives credit to Crum's sister, Catherine Adkins Wicks, who worked alongside Crum in the kitchen. This version of the story goes that she was peeling potatoes and accidentally dropped one of the skins into the hot oil next to where she was working. The crisp result gave her a brilliant idea and eureka! Potato chips.

The invention has also been attributed to several other people over the years. Judging by the fact that both potatoes and oil have been around for a long time, it's likely they have been invented and reinvented several times. Many of those were probably accidents, too.

Commercially, the first potato chips came out of Saratoga Springs, hence the old name "Saratoga Chips." However, although they were produced in Saratoga, they were a gourmet delicacy that was mostly for the wealthy. It was only in the 1930s, when Lays and Fritos started producing their own take on chips, that they become commercially popular and common among the general public. Today, there are hundreds of different brands and flavors of chips.

Potato chips make the world a much tastier place, so it is a good thing a customer complained—or skins were dropped into hot oil—or where would we be otherwise?

POPSICLES

Popsicles are a delicious summer treat that make heat waves bearable and beach days more exciting. It's only right that something so delicious and fun was invented by a kid.

In 1905, Frank Epperson—an 11-year-old boy from San Francisco—was mixing powder and water to make fruit-flavored soda. It was something that he did often, but one night, he didn't finish and left the drink outside with the stirrer still in the cup. That night, it got very cold and the drink froze in the cup.

The next morning, Epperson popped the frozen drink out of the cup and began to lick it. He was stunned by how clever and delicious it was; Epperson had stumbled across something really special.

Over the next couple of years,

he sold his "Epsicles" to kids in his neighborhood over the summers. The name was a combination of his own name, Epperson, and icicle. He continued to sell them around his neighborhood until he decided to upscale his operation to Neptune Beach, where it became a massive success. The treat amazed people with how easy it was to consume right off the stick without the need for any utensils.

Epperson patented the invention in 1924, and the patent even included the best type of wood to use for the sticks. The Epsicle continued to be a great success, and Epperson added many new fruit flavors and sold them all over the country.

The name Popsicle was given to the invention after Epperson's children convinced him that it was much better than Epsicle. The name came from his children calling them Pop's "sicle," which got shortened to Popsicle. The name stuck a lot better than Epsicle, showing once again that children are a great source of ideas.

Popsicles have evolved and adapted over time, and today you can buy many different frozen treats on a stick, not just the frozen fruit juice that it originally was. Whether it is cream-based ice cream or something fruity, eating a frozen treat during the summer is a sure-fire way to help you cool off in the tastiest way possible.

ICE CREAM CONES

Before the edible wafer cone was invented, the only way to serve ice cream was in bowls, which *were* sometimes edible. However, the edible serving dish that was used before the cone was not nearly as easy or fun as our cones are today. It wasn't until the 1904 World's Fair in St. Louis that the cone first became a hit. This World's Fair was a collection of inventions from all over the world—including food—that awarded prizes for the best innovations in specific categories.

The story goes that Syrian immigrant, Ernest A. Hamwi, was selling a crisp waffle-like pastry at the Fair, and he was hoping to do well with his sweet treat. Next to him was another vendor who was selling ice cream. It happened that the vendor had not prepared enough bowls for the quantity of ice cream that he had brought and so thought he wouldn't be able to keep selling his food without something to put the ice cream in.

Thinking fast, Hamwi rolled his pastry into the shape of a cone so that it could hold the ice cream. This new treat was an instant hit and resulted in the two men being the winners of the best food item prize.

Interestingly enough, there is another record of the ice cream cone being invented. In December of 1903, Italo Marchiony was awarded the patent for the brilliant invention of the machine that could make "ice cream cones." But these cones looked nothing like the upside-down party hats that we have today. In fact, a better name for them would have been ice cream bowls, as they were biscuits in the shape of bowls. Even though these did take off in New York, they did not become nearly as popular as the cones from the World's Fair.

It had started as a treat at the fair, but it was about to become an even bigger hit. When the warmer spring weather rolled around in America, concession stands had a new and exciting treat for the public—one they loved and ate up.

There is something rather magical about a cone; some charm that is not carried over to an ice cream sandwich or ice cream bowl. Maybe it's the fun of munching away at the wafer to get more ice cream or the delicate balance of not eating too quickly but eating fast enough that it doesn't get soggy. Either way, the cone really does make eating ice cream more fun than it already is.

CHEESE

For most of human history, refrigeration was not available. Although there were ways to keep certain items cooler, such as storing them underground, the only way to truly preserve food was to dry it, ferment it, or just eat it before it went bad.

People had to plan carefully around the seasons in order to ensure that they had access to food all year-round. Milk presented some difficulties on that front, as it was a fickle substance that was difficult to store and went bad very quickly.

Cheese was a solution to this problem, allowing milk to be stored for longer periods without going bad.

The exact origin of cheese is not known. Some estimates put it as early as 8000 B.C.E. (that's over 10,000 years ago), but it's very unlikely that cheese was intentional. You may have heard that cheese is "off milk," which is not wrong, but it also isn't exactly right. Cheese is *fermented* milk, which means the process is controlled. If you just left milk in the fridge long enough for it to go sour, it is unlikely that it would turn into cheese that wouldn't give you food poisoning.

The most likely story of how cheese was Invented goes a little like this: Cheese came about when sheep were first domesticated. Rennet is the enzyme that results in the formation of cheese and it is found in the stomachs of sheep. Enzymes are substances found in bodies that

help to form new compounds and break down others such as proteins and sugars. We believe that, some 10,000 years ago, , used the stomachs of sheep to store their milk. It was very common at the time for animal organs to be used as water bottles of sorts. The remnants of rennet in these stomach bags combined with hot summer weather, curdled the milk, resulting in the formation of a cheese-like substance.

Salt was added to the curds for further preservation, but even these first cheeses only lasted for a while, and it's unlikely that they were stored for long periods of time. However, as cheese spread across the world, to colder regions, less salt added, which resulted in creamier cheeses that are closer to what we have today.

From sheep stomachs to creamy spreads, cheese has come a long way. It's something that some people love and others hate, but most people have at least one variation that they like. Cheese is a large part of culture and cuisine throughout the world, and although the idea of using a stomach as a storage container may seem strange to us, we can thank this idea for the tasty snack that is cheese.

DONUTS

The only donut without a hole in the middle that I will be eating is a jam donut; it's a personal preference, but anything else is simply not a donut.

Depending on how you define "donut," they have been around for a very long time, but in the beginning they looked very different to the ting that most people picture when they hear the word "donut." This is because they were just round bits of batter that were fried in oil. The name for this sweet treat was not consistent, and there are variations of it found all over the world and in many different cultures.

Donuts were not made with a hole in the middle until 15-year-old Hanson Crockett Gregory and some bad weather at sea changed this completely.

Gregory's mother was known for making delicious olykoek, or "oily cake," and gave some to Gregory for his voyage on a lime-trading ship. She also gave the recipe to the cook, so that he could make the treat for Gregory while they were at sea.

The story goes that Gregory was steering the ship with one hand and had an olykoek in the other when the ship entered a patch of rough sea and high winds. In order to steer better, he grabbed onto the steering wheel with both hands, resulting in the olykoek being impaled on the steering wheel. When the sea was calm once more,

Gregory saw what had become of his snack and decided that he liked it better that way.

For the rest of the trip, he demanded that his chef make the treat with a hole in the middle, and so he did. There are a lot of benefits to cooking the dough with a hole in the middle, including helping it to cook all the way through.

After they returned to shore, this treat quickly caught on, both for its unique look and for how it ensured that never again would you get raw mixture in the center of your fried dough treat.

Today, donuts come in all flavors and colors. Whether it be a simple glaze or covered in sprinkles, there are all sorts of ways to dress them up, as well. However, one thing remains the same—that hole punched straight through the middle is what makes a donut a donut, and it just wouldn't be the same without it.

THE TEA BAG

Tea is probably one of the oldest inventions of all time. It's difficult to pinpoint exactly when it came about, but it's safe to say that it was well over 3,000 years ago. The tea bag, however, is a much more recent invention.

Before the tea bag was invented, people either just drank the tea with all the leaves floating around in the water, or they strained it before drinking it.

So, how was the first tea bag invented? There is some debate as to who actually invented the tea bag, but the most popular story credits the invention to a Thomas Sullivan, in 1906.

Thomas Sullivan was a prominent tea and coffee merchant. He decided to supply samples of his products in small silk pouches, not intending for people to place the pouches directly in water, but rather thinking that they would remove the leaves from the pouch first. A few of his customers tried it that way though, and liked its convenience and how easy it was to use. After that they asked that their tea leaves always be served in small pouches. That way, they would always get the perfect serving size.

However, seven years earlier, Roberta C. Lawson and Mary Molaren of Milwaukee, Wisconsin, applied for a patent for a "tea leaf holder" that resembles what we use today. They wanted something that held the perfect amount of leaves for one cup of tea, minimizing the waste of having to brew an entire pot. They also wanted the design to prevent the leaves from entering the drinker's mouth and to be made of a material that was thin enough to allow the correct diffusion of the leaves' flavor into the drink. They opted for a mesh bag, which held the leaves inside, but which still allowed for all of the flavor to reach the hot water.

Thomas Sullivan later also switched to a mesh material, as the silk threads of his bags were too closely woven and did not allow for an optimal diffusion of the tea, and therefore decreased the flavor.

Regardless of who invented it first, the tea bag solved many of the problems associated with drinking tea at the time; the inability to make a single serving at a time and the messy cleanup of having to wash the leaves out of the pot.

The invention of the tea bag was so simple and ingenious that it has required no modification for a century, and it's safe to say that it will stay that way for a century more.

WORCESTERSHIRE SAUCE

Worcestershire sauce is both a condiment and a word that most people have no idea how to pronounce. Like many condiments, it sits somewhere between a sauce and seasoning and can be left on the shelf for a long time without going bad.

Worcestershire sauce, in case you are wondering what it is, is a dark, almost tar-like sauce that is commonly used in stews and sauces to add a deep, rich flavor. It's quite potent on its own.

The sauce was originally made with malt vinegar, spirit vinegar, molasses, sugar, salt, anchovies, tamarind extract, onions, garlic, and spices. Little has changed from the original recipe to how it is made today. Because why change perfection?

The story of its invention starts with an apothecary. An apothecary is an old term for a pharmacist, but long ago apothecaries did a bit of everything, so it wasn't unusual for them to sell things such as condiments or preserves. Nor was it strange for them to take orders from customers for these sorts of things.

One such apothecary at Lea & Perrins, in Worcester, England, took an order from a customer for a condiment containing the ingredients listed above. The customer, however, forgot to come and collect what they had ordered, so it remained in storage for many months. One day, while a clerk was cleaning out the old and unsold stock in the storeroom, they decided to try the creation. The taste was unique and wonderful, and they realized its potential.

Worcestershire sauce quickly became a hit in both England, where it originated, and in America, although the recipe was changed slightly for American consumers.

It had a unique flavor, but it does have a lot of similarities to many sauces from Europe and farther east—fermented fish. Fermented fish may sound far from enjoyable, but it does have one very important characteristic; it gives food and sauces a very savory taste, which is hard to obtain otherwise.

This savory taste is not something kids are likely to enjoy, but it's something you grow to like over time.

It's a great thing that customer never came to pick up his order, otherwise many dishes would not be the same. They would be a lot blander, and we wouldn't have such a strange word to try to pronounce.

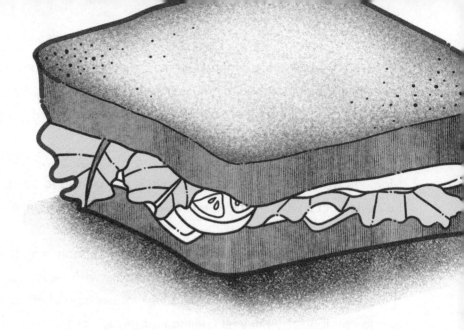

THE SANDWICH

Everyone has had a sandwich at one point or other. Whether it is an iconic PB&J or something as simple as a cheese sandwich, the meal is something that marks so many of our days at school and is considered one of the quickest and easiest snacks to make.

The name "sandwich" comes from John Montagu, who was the fourth Earl of Sandwich in England. That's right, there is actually a place called Sandwich.

Montagu was fond of gambling and got so absorbed in his games that he forgot to eat, because that required him to stop playing. Many of us know the feeling of getting caught up in a good game, book, or TV show, so we can relate to Sir Montagu.

He asked his cook make him a meal that he could eat with his hands and which would not require him to stop his play to do so. The cook's solution was to take a bit of cooked beef and stick it between two pieces of bread. Pretty ingenious.

Montagu was delighted; he did not have to use utensils to eat it, and he could hold it with one hand and keep playing with the other.

Many people saw Montagu eating his sandwich at gambling houses, and not having to stop playing. In time, the sandwich began to spread and it became popular with others for because of how easy it was to eat. It quickly became common for picnics and as finger food at parties, and people experimented with making both savory and sweet sandwiches. It became so popular that "sandwich" became a verb for placing something between two other things.

The first known peanut butter and jelly sandwich recipe was found in a 1901 cookbook. When America started to mass-produce peanut butter, they targeted children, and this was how the PB&J became a staple in many school lunches. Crazy how one little marketing campaign can make something a daily occurrence for many people.

Whether you like it simple and original or get creative with all the wonderful and interesting things you can place between bread, a sandwich is a wonderful thing that makes lunchtime a lot easier.

LiCORiCE

Licorice is something you love to eat or love to hate. It's an incredibly divisive sweet. To the anti-licorice crowd, the sweet is outdated and bitter in comparison to more decadent alternatives. But licorice has a long history, and it starts with plants.

Licorice is a type of candy that gets its name from the licorice plant. The plant has been used for thousands of years to treat all sorts of ailments and, for a long time, was seen as a miracle cure-all. The root of licorice, which is shaped like a potato's root, was made into a tea that was drunk for ulcers and as a cough remedy. The root was later used in the first cough syrup because of its anti-inflammatory effects.

Cough syrup today is not something you would call tasty, and it was even worse back in the day. It was bitter and positively vile. In 1790, a British pharmacist tried to make the syrup a little bit more tolerable, without losing any of its medicinal properties. It makes me think of those sweets that taste more like medicine than candy. He added sugar to the syrup, and the result was a black substance with a tough texture and sweet taste.

It wasn't long before all of Europe was churning out the stuff and selling it to the public.

The treat is especially popular in the northwest European countries of Norway, Sweden, Denmark, Finland, and Iceland, as well as

Germany and the Netherlands. In fact, the sweet is so popular in Sweden that in 2009, they started *Lakritsfestivalen*, a licorice festival that includes tastings, contests, and even sculptures made from licorice.

Over the years, many companies have found ways to dress licorice up and sweeten its originally bitter taste—in the form of "all sorts,"— which are pieces of licorice, covered with very sweet colorful fruit-flavored soft candy. Some companies have chosen to coat licorice in chocolate to mask its taste. Licorice enthusiasts are be amused.

Whether you love or hate it, licorice has a unique flavor all of its own. Nothing in this world has ever come to taste like it. Regardless of how much some people detest it, licorice has remained on the shelves of candy shops and grocery stores for nearly 300 years and will continue to delight and disgust for many more years to come.

RAISINS

Like cheese, raisins, have been around for a long time—over 4,000 years.

Raisins are essentially dried grapes, although you may have thought they were a separate fruit, which is a common misconception. The name "raisin" means "grape" in French, but not that many of us speak French, so that's probably why there was all of that confusion.

They were stumbled upon by complete chance, in Egypt, in roughly 2000 B.C.E.

Egyptian farmers used to grow grapes, and they noticed something strange happened to the grapes that fell off the vines and onto the ground in the hot sun. They dried out and formed strange, darker-colored food that was much much sweeter than a grape was.

The reason for this is that when grapes dry out, the sugar in them crystalizes (becomes more like the sugar you buy in the store and less like a watery syrup) and becomes hard. This loss of water and crystallization results in the sugar becoming more concentrated and thus makes the raisins sweeter.

Still, it's a little surprising that someone would eat something off the ground that looked nothing like a grape, just to see how it tasted.

Oddly enough, it's because of an instinct that humans have; when we encounter something strange or foreign, one of our first responses is to put it into our mouths to figure out what it is. This is why babies put their mouths on everything. This is probably how raisins were discovered. Someone saw them and didn't know what they were, so they ate one.

Because raisins were discovered so long ago, there is no one person to whom we can point to say they discovered them. However, the dried fruit itself has developed a lot since its humble beginnings. Raisins can be made from all kinds of grapes, each of which has its own taste and texture. The method by which they are dried will also determine what the final raisin will taste like. They are very easy to make, and you could even make them at home if you wanted to.

Whether they're part of the trail mix you have for a snack or used for fruit cake at Christmas time, raisins have been around a long time and have found their way into many dishes. They are a great way to sweeten something up in a healthier way than just dumping a bunch of sugar into it.

CHEWING GUM

Some of us like to chew gum to freshen our breath and others like it to blow bubbles, but all of us have felt the shudder run down our spine when our fingers brush against some old chewing gum stuck to the underside of a desk at school.

Chewing gum has been around for a long time, just not in the form that we know it today. In sub-Saharan Africa, the indigenous tribes chewed on the sap of the acacia tree during long journeys. The main ingredient that makes chewing gum chewy comes from a very similar story.

In Mexico, many people were fond of chewing sapodilla sap, which was very chewy, and Antonio López de Santa Anna, an exiled Mexican president, was no different. Santa Anna ended up stuck on Staten Island in New York with no money, so he enlisted the help of a local inventor, Thomas Adams, to try and make the sapodilla sap into a new form of latex. Rubber was booming in America, and he wanted a piece of the action.

Try as he might, Adams could not make the sap into anything that worked as rubber. However, he realized its potential for gum when he saw a little girl order some gum made from paraffin wax, which had a less-than-pleasant taste.

Adams began to turn the sapodilla sap into something that could replace the less satisfying chews that were currently on sale. In 1859, he put the first-ever "chicle balls" on sale, and although they were flavorless, they were an instant hit. Most of the other chewing alternatives had a bitter taste that many people could not stomach, and this new tasteless version was a perfect substitute. Although the thought of chewing a tasteless ball for an extended amount of time does not sound appealing to us now, we wouldn't have chewing gum if there hadn't been something that people liked about chewing those tasteless balls.

Thomas Adams founded what was the largest gum-making company in the world at the time and began to experiment with many different flavors and colors.

Unfortunately, the gum we chew today has little to do with the plants it originally came from. This is due to the overharvesting of the trees and because an artificial gum base was developed. But, whether it's natural or man-made, gum is satisfying to chew and will keep making its way to the underside of school desks.

CHAPTER 3
ACCIDENTALLY LIFESAVING

Where would the world be without modern medicine? The answer is not very far. Medicine has revolutionized the world, helping to increase life spans and to treat diseases that once meant certain death. Most of its beginnings lie in the use of herbs and plants, to treat various ailments, in the form of teas and powders. Today, producing medicine is a multi-billion-dollar industry that sees thousands of chemists and biochemists develop new medicines every year.

What is really interesting about most medical discoveries is they often came from accidents or when people were trying to achieve or figure out something else. They also often came from many different minds over a long period of time. Scientists made amazing discoveries but sometimes they did not know how to harness them or how to make them useful. It took teamwork to make a lot of these inventions and ideas possible. After many years, a new scientist might finally be able to do what the first one never could. Medicine is a true testament to the concept that collaboration is often necessary to get an idea to the finish line.

All of the inventions in this chapter have been helping to save lives and prolong life expectancy since they were first discovered, even if their discovery was completely accidental.

ASPIRIN

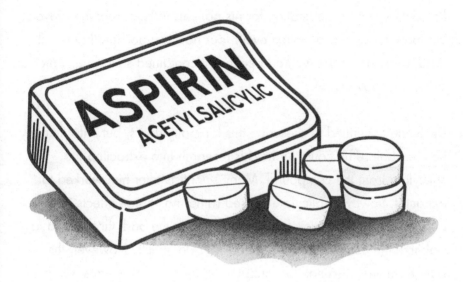

Aspirin is the nickname for acetylsalicylic acid. I know it's a big word, and it's one you will probably never have to remember, unless you plan on becoming a chemist.

Aspirin has been used to treat headaches, arthritis, and many other problems for more than 100 years, due to its strong anti-inflammatory and pain-killing properties. The plant that it is derived from, the willow tree, has been used in herbal medicine since the times of ancient Greece, but it wasn't until 1763 that it was first used in its more purified form.

Reverend Edward Stone fell ill with what may have been malaria and was struggling with fever and pain that came and went. It was during one of these episodes that he accidentally tasted some willow bark. How this bark came to be a part of his diet is unclear, but what is known is that he had a eureka moment as it helped to clear his feverish head.

Stone found that if he dried the bark and crushed it into a powder, he could use it as medication for his patients to help treat their fevers. The powder was to be taken every four hours, a dosage that is still used today. The bark worked because it contained salicylate, which is basically baby aspirin.

Dr. Stone continued to prescribe this for many years, but unfortunately, he died before he could further his research into extracting the salicylate from the compound. Many scientists after him worked to extract it, however salicylate caused rather nasty side effects in its pure form. There was probably something in the bark that helped to stabilize the compound and reduce the side effects. However, the bark form was also not concentrated enough, which means it didn't work as well as it could have.

It wasn't until they were able to create a compound derived from salicylate—acetylsalicylic—that they finally had something that could treat fevers and headaches without the terrible side effects. The successful scientist was called Felix Hoffmann.

Heinrich Dreser, a close associate of Hoffmann, dismissed the market potential of aspirin because it made the heart beat rapidly when taken. Ironically enough, the medicine he was more interested in— heroin— had much worse side effects and was more detrimental to the body than aspirin.

However, Bayer AG, the company where both Hoffman and Dreser worked, saw the potential of the drug and pushed it into production.

Aspirin became a massive success. It is still prescribed today for many different illnesses and pains.

It took accidentally eating bark and the painstaking work of many scientists for it to become a reality. Even though it worked in this instance, eating bark (or anything strange) is not a viable method for finding new medicines, so don't go and taking a bite out of the next tree you see, thinking you will find a cure for a disease.

INSULIN

Diabetes used to be a death sentence for humans. There was almost nothing that could be done to slow it down or to help the body process sugars from carbohydrates (things such as bread, potatoes, and rice). Insulin was the savior, and it was first discovered over 100 years ago.

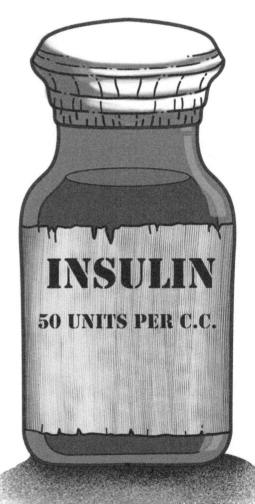

For many years, scientists and doctors were unsure what exactly caused diabetes; they knew all the characteristics of the disease and could easily diagnose it, but without knowing *why* people developed diabetes, doctors struggled to find a cure or even an effective treatment. In order to treat an illness, you have to know why it occurs, or else you are just taking a wild guess.

In 1889, Joseph von Mering and Oskar Minkowski removed the pancreas from a living dog, in order to study the impact of the pancreas on digestion. However, their experiment taught them something very different. The two scientists noticed that the dog started to present with symptoms of diabetes a day after the extraction. They concluded that blood sugar levels were controlled by insulin, a substance produced by the pancreas, but they were unable to isolate the hormone or find any practical use for the substance.

It wasn't until 30 years later that insulin was first isolated and then used to treat diabetes. Sir Frederick G. Banting and Charles H. Best were the first scientists to isolate insulin from one dog and give it to another dog. The results were outstanding as the dog's blood sugar levels quickly returned to normal and the dog was restored to health.

With the help of other scientists, they began to work on developing a purer form of insulin to use on people. On January 11, 1922, the first version of insulin was administered to a 14-year-old boy, and the results were remarkable but not perfect. The scientists continued to refine and improve the insulin until they had the results they wanted— normal blood sugar levels with no obvious side effects, saving the boy and many more to come.

Over the next couple of years, and with the help of many different scientists, insulin was used for a variety of different uses and applications. Insulin, like penicillin, is a testament to how it often takes many minds to make something great. Today, diabetes is more inconvenient than life-threatening when properly managed. It is estimated that nine million people are living healthy lives thanks to this invention (Mond & Proclemer, 2011).

ANESTHESIA

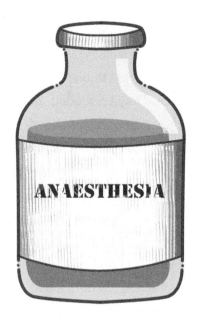

Medical care today would not be the same without anesthetics. From getting a tooth pulled to having major surgery, anesthesia makes many medical procedures bearable.

Anesthesia's first form was nitrous oxide, more commonly known as "laughing gas." This gas is still regularly used in many dental practices.

At an entertainment show in 1844, a dentist named Horace Wells saw another member of the audience, Samuel A. Cooley, inhale the gas as part of the show's act. During the show, Mr. Cooley struck his leg on a bench and started to bleed, but he felt no pain. Wells realized that this was something that the medical community had been looking for, for many years; the ability to numb pain.

Back then, people did not brush their teeth as much as they do now, so this meant that painful tooth extractions were a regular occurrence for many people (we now know that brushing our teeth is very important). Most dentists were constantly looking for ways to improve the experience for their patients and to make these extractions easier.

A little later Wells made a demonstration of nitrous oxide. He tried to pull a tooth from a patient's mouth, but the patient's head jerked back and they howled in pain; a sure sign that the nitrous oxide had not worked. Unfortunately, this was because Wells had not given the patient enough of the anesthetic; however, the doctors watching did not understand this and laughed him out of the operating theater.

It was William Morton who finally gave the first successful demonstration to an audience, using sulfuric ether as opposed to nitrous oxide. Surprisingly, this was not the only exciting thing about Morton's demonstration. He was also the first person to develop a safe way to control and administer the anesthetic to the patient through a mask. This was revolutionary, as all previous attempts ran the risk of overdosing the patients. His invention created a completely new school of medicine: anesthesiology.

Morton, Wells, and Charles Jackson—a chemist who helped Morton with his invention—spent the rest of their lives fighting over who should get the credit, in order to receive all of the wealth that came from such a revolutionary invention. All of them died before the legal battle ended. Sometimes, it is better to just let things go.

Regardless of to whom we owe the credit, anesthesia makes many medical procedures possible. It has also given us many funny videos of people still loopy on it.

THE PACEMAKER

Ever heard "the heart is a fickle thing"? Even though this saying refers to romance, hearts actually can be quite easily disrupted. Sometimes, hearts don't beat as they should and your heart rate can become irregular. This means the time between beats is not regular, which results in a disrupted heart rate that can be life-threatening.

For a long time, there wasn't much that could be done for this condition. We knew why it happened; things such as heart attacks, blockages, and old age can weaken the heart and change a person's heartbeat. However, there was very little that could be done to treat or manage the condition.

As it happened, the person who invented the pacemaker was a "humble tinkerer." Dr. Wilson Greatbatch was an engineer in Clarence, New York. One day he was fiddling with a device in his backyard,

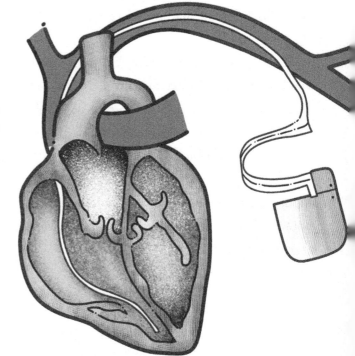

trying to develop a device that could measure the rhythm of a human heart. He was completely focused on the device as he reached into his box of tools for a particular part that completed the circuit. Luckily, he picked up the wrong item and attached it to the circuit. When he did so, the circuit gave off intermittent vibrations, just like a human heart. In other words, the rate at which the device was buzzing was exactly how a human heart should work.

Greatbatch says that he stared at the device in disbelief. He had a eureka moment and instantly realized that this device could be used to drive a human heart. With the help of Dr. William Chardack, a surgeon working at Buffalo's Veterans Administration Hospital, he managed to perfect the device so that it could function inside the human body and not cause any harm to the person wearing it.

Even though they tested the device successfully, Greatbatch was still not satisfied. as it used the batteries that were available at the time, the device had to be replaced every two years. Having that type of major surgery so often was very hard on the body. Dr. Greatbatch obtained the rights to another type of battery and began modifying and perfecting it for use in the pacemaker.

During his lifetime, Greatbatch invented over 300 things, but none was as revolutionary as the pacemaker and the medical batteries that are still used in a number of implants today. He said that he never again felt the same sense of joy as he had when he saw something that he made help a heartbeat, as it did in the first human trials of the device.

Today over one million pacemakers are implanted into people every year, giving them a new chance to live without the constraints of a fickle heart (Mond & Proclemer, 2011).

PENICILLIN

Penicillin was less invented and more discovered, but it is still one of the most vital medical inventions we have today. If it weren't for penicillin, we wouldn't have nearly as many medical treatments and cures as we currently do. The penicillin family makes up a large portion of antibiotics, and penicillin itself is still a very important medication used to treat a number of bacterial infections.

Penicillin was discovered by chance by Sir Alexander Fleming. For a long time, he had been searching to find what he called a "wonder drug"; one that could kill harmful bacteria without damaging the human body. In September 1928, Fleming had just returned from vacation, and was sitting at his workbench at St. Mary's Hospital sorting through a stack of dirty petri dishes. Before he had left, he had stacked up the dishes to clear out some space for another scientist to work at his desk while he was away. Now, he was sorting through the contaminated dishes to see which ones were salvageable.

PENICILLIN

I 000 000 I.E.

While he was placing the contaminated petri dishes into disinfectant, a substance that cleans off and kills bacteria, his former lab assistant, D. Merlin Pryce, walked in. Fleming picked up a petri dish that had not yet reached the disinfectant, to demonstrate how difficult it had in the lab since Pryce had transferred out, and he noticed something interesting on that particular petri dish.

The dish had grown a mold while Fleming was away. This in and of itself was not interesting, but rather the fact that the mold seemed to have killed the *Staphylococcus aureus*—a type of bacteria—that was present on the petri dish was what caught his attention.

Fleming spent the next few months growing mold to isolate which mold or substance had killed the bacteria on the petri dish. With the help of a mycologist (a mold specialist), Fleming determined that the mold was Penicillium and he later named the antibacterial substance penicillin. However, Fleming was not a chemist and was not able to isolate the substance into something useful. Although it was nontoxic and held the antibacterial properties he had been looking for, to Fleming this was not his "wonder drug."

Twelve years later, two scientists, Howard Florey and Ernst Chain, started investigating penicillin. They developed a brown powder that retained its antibacterial properties for more than a few days and was nontoxic; thus, the first antibiotics were born. Because of the Second World War, the substance was mass-produced and it saved countless lives from the infection that can be caused by even the smallest cuts.

Today, we have many different antibiotics for all different types of bacteria—we even have probiotics to protect the good bacteria in our bodies. But if it wasn't for penicillin, a large portion of our medication would not exist.

X-RAYS

X-rays sound so mysterious. This is probably because the scientist who discovered them had no idea what they were and therefore used "X" as a placeholder for what they could be.

The story behind these strange and fascinating waves starts in a laboratory in Wurzburg, Germany. Physicist, Wilhelm Conrad Röntgen, was observing whether or not cathode rays (a type of electrical wave) could pass through glass when he saw that a chemically coated substance began to glow, due to the rays.

Determined to better understand these strange new waves, Röntgen shut himself in his lab and began conducting a series of tests. What he found was revolutionary: X-rays are very similar to light rays but much, much smaller. They were able to pass through human flesh but not more solid things such as bone and lead.

Even better, the rays could be photographed.

For the first time in medical history, doctors could see inside the human body without having to cut someone open. Pretty awesome.

This new diagnostic tool was first used in military hospitals where the machine could be used to identify broken bones and bullets still in the body. X-rays moved on to be used in hospitals all over the world, but unfortunately doctors did not understand how harmful they could be.

High exposure to this type of radiation can result in burns, tissue damage, and even cancer. It was only after the death of Clarence Dally, Thomas Edison's assistant, who worked extensively with X-rays and who died from skin cancer, that people started taking the danger seriously. But it took another 30 years before safe X-ray practices were put into place.

People were so casual about it that you could have your feet X-rayed in shoe stores while your shoes were being fitted. Imagine getting an X-ray while shopping at the mall. It seems crazy. Today, people who work with X-rays have to wear heavy protective equipment, and a doctor will only expose you to the rays if it is necessary and in a very controlled and limited manner.

Regardless of how dangerous they can be, X-rays were what paved the way for CT scans, MRIs, and all the other forms of imaging that show us what goes on beneath the skin. Next time you need an X-ray, remember that it all came from an accident and scientists who were determined to understand why.

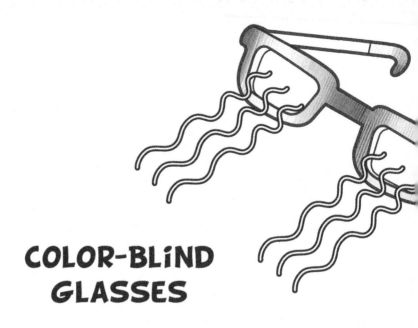

COLOR-BLIND GLASSES

The world is a beautiful place. From blue skies to green grass, it is a place full of color and things that catch the eye. But what if it wasn't? Some people's view of the world is dulled due to them not being able to see certain shades of color.

We see color due because white light is composed of seven different frequency ranges that our eyes process and interpret. It sounds very complicated, but think of it like a supermarket. Colors are all the different items in the market and your eyes are free to "buy" whichever items they find. This results in you seeing the colors that you do. But some people's supermarkets do not stock some of the items—some of the colors—and therefore they cannot buy them. These people are called color-blind.

Granted, they can still *see* color. I used to think being color-blind meant you saw the world like those old black-and-white movies, but no. Color-blind people *can* see color; however, they can only see particular colors.

The first glasses to correct this condition were invented by Don McPherson. But when he invented them, he was not thinking about color-blind people at all. Instead, McPherson was trying to develop protective eyewear for surgeons who used lasers (what an incredibly specific purpose).

He had noticed that the lenses helped to improve colors and made them "pop", but he didn't realize how amazing they were until he gave them to his friend to try on. His friend stared through the glasses in amazement as he was able to differentiate an orange cone in a grassy green field, which he had not been able to do moments ago. His friend was red-green color-blind—a type of color blindness that affects a person's abilities to see shades of red and green accurately. With the glasses on, he was seeing the world in full color for the first time in his life. It was this moment that made McPherson suddenly realize that the lenses could be much more beneficial to the public than they could to specialized surgeons.

Over the next couple of years, he acquired grants to develop the lenses further and researched the technology, which got to the point where it could seamlessly correct red-green color blindness.

Today, thousands of people are able to see the world more vividly thanks to these lenses. There are many heartwarming videos on the internet that show people seeing color for the first time.

Although these lenses currently only treat red-green color blindness, it does present exciting opportunities for potentially correcting the other rarer forms of color blindness. Unless you see the world like the old black-and-white movies—there isn't much we can do for that.

VASELiNE

Today, we use Vaseline for everything from dry lips and skin to treating wounds in hospitals and preventing hair dye stains. Vaseline is made from petroleum jelly, a naturally occurring substance that is found in the ground.

In 1859, oil was in high demand. Being able to successfully mine and sell it meant getting rich quickly. Robert Chesebrough was like anyone else and wanted to find wealth and live a comfortable life. He believed that he could join the oil race to do this, but the land he purchased to harvest oil did not turn out to be very profitable.

One day, he went to check on how his workers were doing, but was met with complaints. The workers had not been able to find oil; instead, they had only stumbled across an annoying waxy substance that clogged up their drills and prevented them from making any progress in their search for oil. This substance was petroleum jelly, but the workers called it "rod wax" because it clogged the rods used to drill for oil.

Not willing to lose all the money he had put into the project, Chesebrough decided to investigate the substance further. He noticed how the workers used this "rod wax" on the small cuts and burns they got while working. Suddenly, the substance was not a mere annoyance but could be used for something.

Chesebrough decided to name the substance Vaseline and marketed it as a healing ointment for small household wounds.

Vaseline has many more uses than just helping to soothe small injuries. There is a reason it is so widely used in hospitals. Whether it be eczema, dry skin, brittle nails, or dry pet paws, petroleum jelly is a suitable remedy. The reason it is so beneficial is that it traps the moisture that is often lost when you have a wound or burn under the skin.

Petroleum jelly is also very stable, which means that it doesn't cause irritation or allergic reactions as many other healing ointments can.

Even though Robert Chesebrough was not able to join the oil race, he was able to market and sell something that is very useful to many people. A lot of people would still have dry, irritated skin if it were not for his quick thinking and accidental find. It turned out that the patch of land was profitable after all.

CHAPTER 4
ACCIDENTALLY AROUND THE HOUSE

Many things make our lives easier and simpler around our homes. Whether it is electricity or running water, we live our lives with many more conveniences than our ancestors did. Every day, we use many items without ever wondering how they came to be and or how they made their way into our homes.

Houses are an invention themselves, and almost everything in them had to be invented at some point as well. Our homes are teeming with the results of the ideas and hard work of others. Because we often do not know where they come from, we miss out on their amazing stories.

In every house, there is also that drawer that is filled with things that we might need one day; stashed away for when we inevitably do need them, and then we have to sift through everything until we find what we need. Many of the inventions in this chapter will end up in that drawer.

This chapter is all about the things that make daily life easier or sit in the drawer unused until their time comes to shine.

SAFETY PINS

Safety pins are one of those things that we can go years without needing and then suddenly we are rummaging through our drawers trying to find one. Parents often use them to temporarily tailor our clothes to fit as we grow. They stand with the pin in their mouth saying, "It *will* fit, eventually!"

The safety pin was originally invented by Walter Hunt in 1849 (that's right, it's been around for over 150 years!). Hunt was a prolific inventor, but still struggled to put food on the table and to provide for his family. This was largely due to his selling his ideas before they became mainstream and therefore not making much profit from them.

He got the idea for the safety pin as he was pacing the floor, worried about how he was going to pay off all his debt. He was winding a piece of wire around his finger when the idea came to him. What if there was a pin that could be worn for long periods of time without the risk of its poking you? A safe pin?

Hunt came up with the idea to encase the pointed side in a cap and attach the pin to a spring so that it could be easily removed from the cap when it needed to be. Sadly, his timeless invention did not put him in a path to riches as many might have thought.

After procuring the patent for the invention, he sold it on, for about $10,000 in today's money and used it to pay off his debt. Although Hunt was a brilliant inventor—he came up with many important inventions, such as the sewing machine—he lacked an understanding of business. This resulted in some of his inventions being stolen so others could profit from them, and his selling off his ideas before he could start to make any real money from them. He would have done a lot better if he'd had a good business partner or sought advice on how to market and sell his products.

Sadly, such a brilliant mind is not remembered as are other inventors, but we can still be grateful for what he invented. Even with Velcro and elastic now being commonplace, safety pins still have their place in the world, either for practical uses or for fashion. Next time you use a safety pin, remember the name Walter Hunt, a brilliant mind that has gone unrecognized for far too long.

VELCRO

Whether you are happily pulling Velcro apart and re-sticking it or frustratingly pulling fluff out of it, you may have found yourself wondering how it works, at some time.

Velcro is a temporary way of keeping things together. You don't have to sew your clothes together, which is difficult to do, you can just use a bit of Velcro. Velcro came along after safety pins, and it is much less limited in its uses.

George de Mestral was hiking in Switzerland one day with his dog, when he noticed something interesting. His dog's fur and his clothes were covered in burs, a type of seed that easily sticks to clothes and hair. Rather than being annoyed, de Mestral was fascinated. What enabled the burs to stick to his clothes so easily?

He took a few burs home and looked at them under the microscope. He saw how they had hook-like structures that allowed them to hook onto nearly any type of fabric or hair. De Mestral realized that this was a great new way to fasten things, somewhere between buttons, zippers, and sewing. He began working to craft a synthetic version of the burs.

The idea was to have one side that had the burr-like hooks and the other side that had loops of fabric, which the hooks could latch onto. If all went well, they would come together simply.

The problem was finding a fabric that worked well for the job. He looked all over Europe before he found a mixture of nylon and cotton that worked perfectly. He managed to make the first piece of Velcro and to get it patented. Them, he was presented with another challenge. The Velcro had to be handmade, and de Mestral could not think of a way to mass-produce it. With much trial and error, he finally developed a machine that could make Velcro.

Nearly twenty years after he first had his idea, Velcro hit the market, but it didn't sell. It wasn't easy to convince the public of its uses, and it might have never become a success if it hadn't been for NASA.

NASA needed something to keep tools in place in space, where there was no gravity to keep things down. Velcro was perfect. Due to space being exciting and cool, Velcro, too, became cool. It quickly made its way onto clothing, even high-end fashion.

Nature is a great place to find inspiration. The Velcro company continues to use this idea to come up with new and exciting inventions.

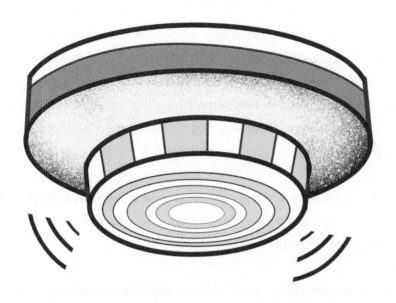

SMOKE DETECTORS

Fires are scary and can be extremely dangerous. What if you didn't know there was a fire until it was literally at your feet? Before smoke detectors and other fire prevention systems, this is how it was. Fire was random, and there was little that could be done to stop it before it got out of hand.

Smoke detectors have saved many lives since their invention and have also reduced how damaging fires can be. However, the device was never meant to be for smoke but rather for poisonous gas.

Swiss scientist, Walter Jaeger, had an idea that he could build a device that would alter an electrical current when poisonous gas entered a system, thus setting off an alarm. The problem was poisonous gas did not activate the alarm. Frustrated that all of his work was wasted and that he would have to start again, he lit a cigarette and noticed in amazement how the smoke from the cigarette triggered the system. Surprised and excited, Jaeger suddenly realized a new potential for his device and began working to perfect it.

Smoke is a lot more common in homes and businesses than poisonous gas, which means this new device was much more likely to sell to the general public than his original idea.

A couple of years later, another Swiss scientist specialized the device for the types of gases found in mines. Ernst Meili was the scientist to do this, and he also made the original smoke detector a lot more sensitive and, therefore, more effective.

Today, there are a wide variety of smoke detectors and thy are used for many things. There are the household ones that many of us have in our homes, which are designed to have a sensitivity specifically to smoke. There are the ones used in big buildings that often trigger fire defense systems such as sprinklers or sprinklers that contain the same substance as fire extinguishers. Now, there are even devices that detect poisonous gas in chemical labs.

Whether it be for poisonous gas or smoke, these devices are lifesaving and have completely changed how we deal with and manage fire.

TEFLON

You might be wondering what in the world Teflon is. Well, it's a substance that is used to coat pots and pans to make them nonstick. Of course, this isn't its only use, but it is the most notable one.

Teflon was invented by Dr. Roy Plunkett in 1938, while he was working at the DuPont chemistry lab. He was trying to make a less toxic refrigerant than the ones that were available at the time. A refrigerant is a substance that makes a refrigerator produce cold air.

He was testing out tetrafluoroethylene as an alternative. With the help of his assistant, he created the chemical and stored the gas in small cylinders that were then frozen. When they tried to get the gas out of the cylinders, nothing came out. The cylinders could not have been empty because they still weighed the same. Deciding to investigate further, the men cut the cylinders open and found a waxy white resin inside.

After running some tests, they discovered that this resin had four very useful properties. It was very slippery, noncorrosive, chemically stable, and only melted at incredibly high temperatures. Understanding that there was great potential in the substance, Dr. Plunkett sent it to the research development team that specialized in polymers (the type of substance the waxy resin was).

It took three more years before it was patented and another four before it was used in industry and the military. It wasn't until the 1960s that it was used in its most well-known role—on nonstick pans. There is a very long list of other uses for Teflon, as it has applications in most things due to its properties, and we continue to find new uses for it.

Cooking with a nonstick pan makes cooking healthier as one needs less oil and it makes the cleanup easier, as whatever is left on the pan just slides right off. Teflon also makes pans cheaper because you do not have to buy expensive cast-iron ones to get a nonstick pan. Teflon is beneficial in many aspects of our lives, and it is all thanks to someone's accidentally freezing a gas.

MICROWAVE OVENS

When microwave ovens first came onto the commercial market, a lot of people were very scared of them. Today, they are so common that it would be strange not to have one in your home. You are also probably safer standing next to your microwave than outside during a lightning storm.

Microwave ovens did not come out of trying to find a new way to cook food but rather out of attempts to improve communications and radars. Percy Spencer, a self-taught engineer, was the person who realized the kitchen potential of

microwaves. One day, he was working with a magnetron, when he noticed that the peanut cluster bar in his pocket had melted. This was very unusual and prompted him to keep testing.

He went on to expose other foods

to the magnetron's radiation to see what would happen. To his delight, an egg started to violently shake before exploding onto his face. The next day he was able to cook popcorn for the whole office using the device. Not only could he cook food using this method, but he could also do it a lot faster than traditional ovens or stoves.

Spencer did not know whether the microwave ovens were safe or not, but seeing as he had worked in a lab all the time with microwaves, he didn't think that there was much of a risk. Today, we know that the low levels of radiation a microwave oven gives off are not harmful to humans and do not make our food any less nutritious.

The first microwaves that hit the market were not well received for two reasons. Firstly, the technology was new and revolutionary, which made microwave ovens extremely expensive. Secondly, people were very unsure and often afraid of them, so they did not purchase them.

The inventions really only took off in 1967. By 1975, over a million microwaves were being sold every year, and today over 90% of American households contain a microwave (Liegey, 2017). Microwaves make heating up food quick and easy and ensure that you always get the perfect movie theater popcorn at home.

From studying waves to cooking food, they certainly are a strange invention that is very helpful to us.

MATCHES

Before the modern-day friction-type matches, lighting fires was a hassle and often took a lot of time and patience.

A British pharmacist, John Walker, changed all of this. He was working on an experimental paste that could be used in a similar way to gunpowder but which he hoped would be more effective. While he was working, he used a small piece of wood to mix all the substances in the paste. He struck this wood against the workbench he was working at and was amazed when it caught fire.

This little moment gave him a brilliant and exciting idea. Perhaps there was a better way to light a fire. With some modification and testing, he perfected the sticks by using a paste of antimony sulfide, potassium chlorate, and gum arabic. The cardboard sticks were dipped into sulfur. He first started selling these "friction lights" out of his pharmacy, on April 12, 1827. He later used hand-cut wooden splinters for the sticks and then eventually packaged them into cardboard boxes with a little bit of sandpaper on the side for easy striking. His invention quickly became popular for its ease of use and how much it cut down the time it took to light a fire.

Walker was strongly advised to patent his invention, but for whatever reason, he chose not to, and a short time later, in 1829, Samuel Jones of London started selling his "Lucifers," which were an identical copy of Walker's invention.

Matches spread quickly across
England, and soon there were
hundreds of factories popping up all over
the country to satisfy people's desire for the small fire-starting sticks.

Originally, mass-produced matches were made with white
phosphorus, which is quite a toxic chemical. The people who
worked in these factories—primarily women and children—were at
a very high risk of developing "phossy jaw," which is damage to
the jawbone due to phosphorus exposure. The illness was incredibly
painful and resulted in many people losing their jobs and their lives.

It took nearly 80 years for the use of white phosphorus to be
outlawed in the production of matches. Today, matches are nontoxic
and a lot safer than their original brothers and sisters; but even then,
they were revolutionary for daily life.

POST-iT NOTES

Whether you are using them to stick reminders up on your desk or to mark important information in a book, Post-it notes are a simple yet useful item. The invention of these little squares can be attributed to two people: Dr. Spencer Silver and Art Fry.

Dr. Silver was a 3M scientist, working on developing tougher and stronger adhesives that would be useful for multiple industrial purposes. As he was experimenting, he stumbled across something quite the opposite. The adhesive he happened to make was neither strong nor tough. This was obviously considered a failure in the eyes of the lab, but Silver didn't feel this way because to one very important thing; his adhesive could be reused.

If the adhesive was placed on paper and the paper was stuck to something, it could be pulled off without causing any damage to the paper or the other surface. The paper could then easily be re-stuck and retained its adhesive properties. This was a one-of-a-kind adhesive, but Dr. Silver could not find a use for it, at first.

It wasn't until a couple of years later that the end idea struck and stuck. A man called Art Fry was getting frustrated with using bits of paper to mark the hymns he needed to sing in his bible, as they kept falling out. He wanted to find something that he could stick to the pages without damaging them.

He suddenly remembered a seminar he had attended from Dr. Silver and realized that the strange adhesive was exactly what he was looking for. Teaming up, the two began to develop the Post-it note. However, it did not attract much public interest when they first released it, in 1977. It took a massive marketing campaign to get this little invention to take off.

Today, the notes are posted all over offices, homes, and books, and many people would not be able to work without these little reminders. From not-quite-right to simply perfect, Post-it notes have not changed all that much over the years—a mark of how ingenious they are.

PLASTiC

Plastic is one of those things that is everywhere, all the time. From water bottles to phone cases, it would be difficult to count all of the things in our lives that are made out of plastic. Synthetic plastic has been around for over 100 years and it was originally called Bakelite.

Bakelite was discovered by Leo Hendrik Baekeland in 1907, while he was trying to come up with a cheaper alternative to shellac, which is a kind of resin or varnish. During the process, he mixed a few different substances together and the result wasn't what he was looking for.

The resulting substance was a type of polymer (a special group of chemicals that most types of plastic are made out of) that did not melt under heat or stress. This was unusual compared to the polymers that were available at the time, and it presented a new opportunity for synthetic materials.

Most synthetic materials back then were designed to mimic natural materials, but so they could be produced at a lower cost. This new thermosetting plastic changed that. The substance didn't need to mimic the natural world; it could stand on its own and worked even better than the natural materials that were available.

This was instrumental to future research into synthetic substances, as it meant that we were no longer restricted to mimicking nature, but could make anything from our wildest dreams as long as we got the chemistry right.

It might not sound all that interesting, but it changed how people thought about the research process, shifting it to be more independent and more innovative.

Today, we use Bakelite for everything from phones to jewelry to clocks. We also have a much larger range of plastics of different thicknesses, properties, and polymers than we initially had, all of which would have not been possible without the invention of Bakelite.

Plastic sent the world into a craze for synthetic materials, because of cheap it was to produce and how much we could do with so little. It's a craze we are yet to overcome.

PAPER TOWELS

What would a kitchen be without paper towels? Paper towels are a quick and easy way to clean up messes in the kitchen, especially if they involve some kind of liquid. They are also used in public bathrooms as a more sanitary way to dry our hands.

Before paper towels, bathrooms had regular hand towels in them that everyone used. The problem with this was that it was an easy way to pass on germs. If one person was sick and used the towel, there was a risk that those germs would be passed on to the next person who used the towel. Paper towels solved this problem.

Arthur Scott invented paper towels because of an accident with a shipment. Scott ran a toilet paper factory and was brought a shipment of paper that was much too thick for toilet paper. Rather than discard the mistaken shipment, Scott had an idea.

He had heard about a teacher in a primary school who had given children who were sick soft paper to use rather than the communal towels in the bathrooms, so that they didn't make the other children sick. Amazingly it had worked, and Scott now had a use for his mistaken delivery.

The rejected toilet paper was cut into pieces that were a little bit smaller than hand towels and marketed as disposable paper towels. They capitalized on the idea of their being more sanitary than

ordinary towels and people were encouraged to use them as single-use items. They were an instant success and helped to reduce the spread of colds and the flu.

A couple of years later, Scott developed a paper towel for the kitchen, which is where it is used most often today. It took a little longer for people to trust paper kitchen towels, but soon they were regular items in most people's homes.

There are many uses for paper towels and their most important task is ensuring our bathrooms and kitchens stay clean and germ-free.

CHAPTER 5
ACCIDENTALLY INDUSTRIAL

In order for industry to exist, we need inventors. In fact, industry would become stagnant if it was not for the constant evolution and development of new products and ideas. Whether it be a new type of plastic, a faster computer chip, or a synthetic fabric, industry thrives on the creative thinking that is required for innovation.

"Industry" is basically all of the businesses that provide the products and services we buy and use in our daily lives, but it also includes things that are produced on a very large scale or are used for less-simple things—such as explosives or the metals used in building big machines for mining or farming. All of the inventions in this chapter have helped to grow and develop industry in one or more ways.

DYNAMITE

Dynamite is good for more than just cool explosions in movies, although that is an added bonus. Before dynamite, there was no "commercial" means to safely blast things, and there was very little we could do in terms of making things explode.

This meant that building bridges, demolishing buildings, and mining all had to be done by hand. This was time-consuming, dangerous, and expensive. Many scientists had investigated explosives, and the first one was discovered, by accident, by Christian Friedrich Schönbein in 1835.

Schönbein was experimenting with sulfuric and nitric acid in his kitchen, when he accidentally spilled the mixture. Thinking quickly, he used his wife's cotton apron to mop up the mixture. When he hung the apron by the stove to dry, it suddenly burst into flames and completely disappeared. Schönbein realized that it was the cellulose in the cotton that had reacted with the acids and caused the explosion.

Then, Ascanio Sobrero developed the technology further when he replaced cellulose with glycerine, a similar chemical. The result was a substance known as nitroglycerine. Nitroglycerine is highly volatile in its raw state; in simple terms, that means that it makes things go "boom" really easily.

Alfred Nobel finally formulated nitroglycerine into a usable state that became what we know today as dynamite. Nobel mixed the liquid with silica and made a malleable paste that still retained the explosive properties but which was much more controllable. This substance was called dynamite.

Nobel improved blasting technology and patented several inventions, including blasting gelatin and the blasting cap, which enabled dynamite explosions to go off more smoothly and effectively. He started a company that produced large amounts of nitrocellulose and nitroglycerine. Later, he also founded the Nobel Prize, one of the most well-known awards for scientists and academics.

From a kitchen accident to mines and rock blasting, as well as jaw-dropping action films, dynamite has come a long way. It's a good thing that the apron was at hand and that the explosion was not so big that the entire house went in flames.

Today, this invention is truly booming.

SAFETY GLASSES

Most protective things in life come after something bad happens. Seat belts were invented after thousands of people had been thrown out of cars during accidents. Even precautions with X-rays only came 50 years after their invention, when people began to die of skin cancer. Safety glasses are no different.

If you have never been in a lab, you might not know what dangerous places they are and what the appropriate attire is. Scientists working in labs have to wear gloves, lab coats, and goggles in order to protect themselves. Depending on their work, they might even need to wear hazmat suits. Goggles are worn to protect the eyes from chemical splashes or vapors that may burn the eyes, and they are used by many different industries to protect workers' eyes.

Safety glasses came from the invention of safety glass. In 1903, French scientist, Edouard Benedictus, was working in the lab when he accidentally knocked over a glass flask containing cellulose nitrate. To his amazement, the pieces of glass did not completely shatter. Although the flask had broken, the pieces still retained their shape due to a plastic-like film that the cellulose nitrate had coated the glass.

He had also read how car accidents resulted in terrible injuries from shattered glass and believed that this film could make glass safer and therefore accidents less deadly. This was the world's first safety glass.

Julius King was the first person to modify safety glass technology into protective eyewear. King was an eye specialist and was very concerned about the eye injuries that people working in certain industries sustained. he worked together with the American Optometric Association to develop the first pair of safety glasses. They later released goggles that could also be used by workers working in hot environments, such as metal works and furnaces.

The safety glasses we have today are now made of protective plastic as opposed to safety glass and have a whole range of other features, such as being antifog. But, if it hadn't been for a slip of the hand, safety glass would never have been discovered and safety glasses would not have been possible.

VULCANIZED RUBBER

In case you are just as confused about what vulcanized rubber is as I was when I first heard about it, let me give you a little run down. Vulcanized rubber is just stronger rubber. The properties that make rubber such a desirable material are improved through the use of heat and sulfur and the result is a stronger, tougher rubber, which we call "vulcanized." It's like giving rubber superpowers.

Charles Goodyear was the brain behind the vulcanization process so that rubber can be used in industry. Goodyear was trying to find a

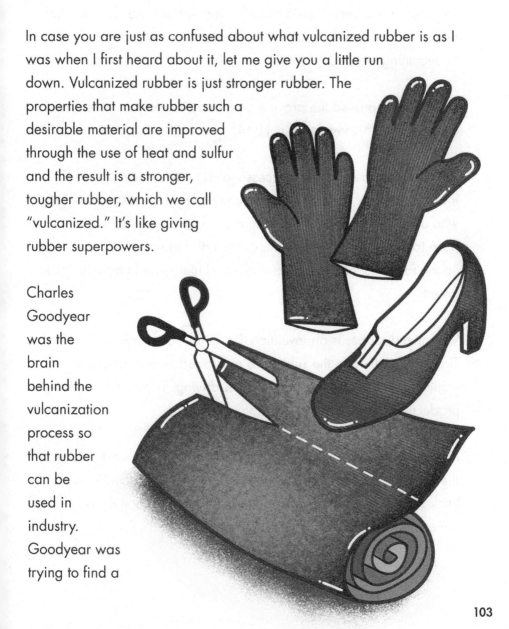

process that would make India rubber non-sticky and resistant to very high and very low temperatures. His first version proved useless at high temperatures.

He had learned, from Nathaniel M. Hayward, that rubber that was treated with sulfur was no longer sticky, but the process to make rubber resist changes in temperature came about by accident, when he dropped rubber mixed with sulfur onto a hot stove. The resulting rubber was less likely to break under pressure and was more resistant to becoming warped.

Goodyear improved the process and made it more controlled, and then patented his invention in 1844.

Unfortunately, he had little success making any money out of his invention. In fact, he spent his life fighting legal battles with people who used his invention without purchasing the rights (something you have to do when an invention is patented) and so he struggled to set up the factories that would have allowed him to profit from his own invention.

Vulcanized rubber is an invention that helps our everyday lives. Tires are made from the substance as rubber, in its normal state, would warp and melt while a car was driving. This is due to the heat produced from the spinning motion.

Many people made millions from his discovery, but Goodyear himself died penniless and in debt. Even though we cannot pay Goodyear back for his ingenuity and hard work, the least we can do is remember his name.

SMART DUST

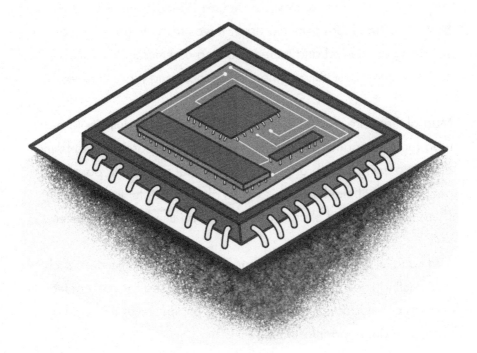

Chances are you've never heard of smart dust. Due to its very specialized use, it's not exactly a household item.

Smart dust has to do with computer chips and programming. You could ask, when are any of us going to need a computer chip that is only a millimeter big? Although it may be a subject that goes over most of our heads, it's still something very interesting and is one of the most recent inventions in our list.

Smart dust was invented by Jamie Link, a graduate student at the University of California, in 2003. Link was trying to coat a much larger chip in a silicone film and broke a piece of the chip off by mistake. She noticed that the smaller chip still retained the properties of the original chip.

Her observations led to the discovery of smart dust. Link could have very well brushed the mistake aside and started over, but she chose to be curious and learn from her error. It was revolutionary. Research is still being conducted and there is nothing commercially available that contains smart dust yet, but the ideas concerning it are very exciting.

Most of them are related to the medical field as the dust could be used for better administration of medication. Research is also being done into using it for brain manipulation that could help paralyzed people use artificial limbs (this would also be helpful to amputees). There is also a good chance that it could be used to treat cancer.

Additionally, there are some military applications of the dust, such as detecting toxic chemicals, which could be used for early detection of chemical warfare. It also has exciting prospects for the wireless transfer of data and information.

Even though it's very unlikely that we will have smart dust lying around our homes any time soon, it is still an exciting and interesting invention. Its discovery shows us that mistakes are not something that we should hide or sweep under the rug. Next time you make a mistake, look a little deeper—you might have discovered something that could change the world.

KEVLAR

You probably do know what Kevlar is, you probably just don't know it's called Kevlar. The coolest use of Kevlar is in bulletproof vests. Kevlar is a synthetic substance that is heat resistant and very strong. Hence the whole bullet-stopping thing.

Stephanie Kwolek, the inventor of Kevlar, loved to mix science and sewing. A seemingly unrelated combination, she started experimenting with fabrics from a young age and discovered a passion for chemistry and medicine while at university.

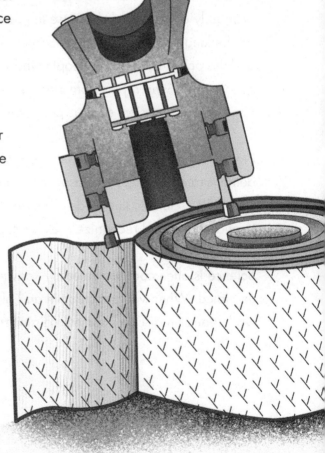

It wasn't long before Kwolek became fascinated with polymers. We have mentioned polymers before, and they are a group of chemicals that form long chains. Kwolek specifically liked to work with them at low temperatures, and it was when she was observing these that she stumbled across something incredible. The material was incredibly strong and stiff, something that could have been missed if she hadn't been paying such close attention.

This discovery was revolutionary; it was a plastic that was five times stronger than steel and was the strongest synthetic substance ever created. In fact, it was so unique that its discovery led to an entirely new industry, which has produced more than 200 new items. Not only is it good for stopping bullets, but it is also used in spaceships, space suits, boats, car brakes, fiber-optic cables, and even shoes.

The substance is also being used in fashion for protection, but it's incredibly pricey. This is because the people buying the clothes are looking for safety, not style. It's not just used by the military and the police but also by people who work dangerous jobs, such as journalists who report from war zones or people who may be targeted by assassins, such as politicians.

Not only did Kwolek discover something amazing, but she also demonstrated an important aspect of science; mixing and matching. Due to her scientific knowledge and her love of sewing she was able to understand and recognize uses for the substance.

Science is often complemented by knowledge that is completely unrelated. When you get creative and play with what can and can't work, you can discover something amazing. Kevlar is a testament to this.

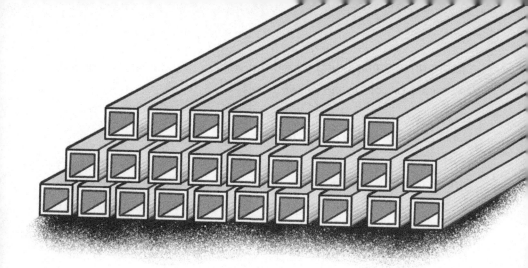

STAINLESS STEEL

Steel has been around for a long time, and no one knows exactly who invented it. It is made by adding carbon to iron, which results in a substance that is much stronger and tougher than either carbon or iron alone. However, one big problem exits with steel—it contains iron and iron rusts.

Unlike other metals, iron rust does not create a protective layer around itself that prevents further damage. When iron rusts, it disintegrates. It is slowly eaten away until it is nothing but dust. Adding carbon to this does not stop the process of rust.

The method of overcoming this frustrating problem was first discovered in 1821, by Pierre Berthier. He added chromium—another metal—to iron and this prevented its rusting. However, no one could find the suitable ratio of chromium to iron, so that wouldn't result in a very brittle substance that had no use. Despite many people's trying and many patents being issued, no version of the mixture was ever marketed or sold to the public.

Until Harry Brearley came along.

Brearley was working on developing a metal alloy that was strong enough for the barrel of a gun. It was tedious work that took months. As the pile of scrap metal next to his workstation began to rust, he realized something very strange. One of the test barrels was still gleaming; it had not rusted like the others. When Brearley tried to test the barrel to see what its composition was, he realized that it was very resistant to chemicals as well. Luckily, he was able to identify what the composition was and, three weeks after his initial discovery, he had perfected the alloy.

At that time, the company that Brearley worked for made mostly cutlery, and he realized that this new "rustless steel" would be perfect for that use. Cutlery was usually made out of steel or silver. Steel was tedious to maintain and silver was too expensive for most people. This was a perfect solution.

A friend at the company agreed with him and they named the material "stainless steel." Soon, they were starting the world's first stainless steel company and mass-producing the stuff by the ton.

Thanks to Brearley's find, we no longer have to constantly polish and take care of our steel items. Imagine how much time this has saved us!

CHAPTER 6
ACCiDENTALLY ACCiDENTAL

Sometimes, things don't quite fit into just one category or it is difficult to place them anywhere. This chapter is all about inventions that could fit into many chapters or none at all. Whether it's something that can be used in industry, around the house, or even everywhere, this is the section where you'll find them!

They are just as accidental and as exciting, but they are what I call miscellaneous.

BUBBLE WRAP

We've all popped Bubble Wrap before. Whether you jumped on it, twisted it between your hands, or painstakingly popped each individual bubble, you know what it is. Bubble Wrap is sometimes more exciting than the thing that is wrapped in it. It is also very important in the shipping world, as it reduces the risk of breakage. It has also allowed online shopping to become as common as it is today.

Alfred Fielding and Marc Chavannes invented Bubble Wrap. However, they were trying to invent a textured wallpaper. To do this, they put sheets of plastic shower curtains through a device that bound them together; however, the results were more than disappointing.

The sheets became covered

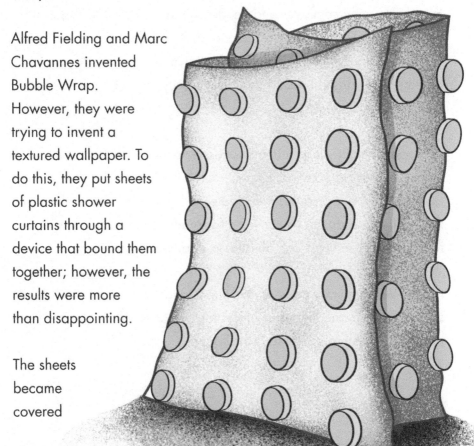

in air bubbles, which was the last thing they had been expecting. Even though it was not what they wanted, they did not dismiss the invention outright. They patented it and became the first people to create a process for embossing and laminating.

After they had secured the patent, they started to think of uses for their invention. They managed to come up with over 400 uses, and many of them were as successful as the textured wallpaper.

In 1960, they founded the Sealed Air Corporation and one year later that they started using their "Bubble Wrap" in packaging. It was here that they found success.

The idea for using it as packaging came about because IBM had launched a new computer and needed a way to safely transport it without the risk of its being damaged. In those days, computers were the size of a room and incredibly expensive. If the computer was damaged in transit, it would be a very pricey fix. Bubble Wrap was the perfect solution.

This opened the eyes of many businesses to the product, and it quickly began to grow in popularity. It was particularly useful for small businesses whose previous only choice for protecting their deliveries was with newspapers, which wasn't very effective. A high rate of return on broken items can be fatal to small businesses.

Bubble Wrap quickly came in all shapes and sizes, and today, it is still the number one means of protecting goods in shipping. Still, if you ask me, its real purpose is for popping.

WiRELESS INTERNET

Where would be without the internet? From video games to Netflix, all is possible only because of the internet. The internet we use today runs on Wi-Fi, a wireless technology that is used to connect computers. Before Wi-Fi, you had to connect to the World Wide Web (the early internet) through a series of cables and dial-ups, but Wi-Fi made connection faster and simpler. In fact, without it, smartphones wouldn't be very smart.

John O'Sullivan, an Australian engineer, was not trying to create a new way to connect to computers and the World Wide Web; rather, he was trying to listen to black holes. The phrase "listen" is used loosely here, as he was trying to develop a way to observe the waves released by black holes.

He had been inspired by Stephen Hawking's theory of evaporating black holes and their radio waves. On his quest, he discovered some radio waves that were much weaker than the other radio waves of the universe. He and his team of researchers set out to develop a device that could identify and filter these radio waves so that they could be observed without the other waves interfering. Unfortunately, they were not able to find the black hole's waves.

A few years later, O'Sullivan was tasked by SCIRO (the Commonwealth Scientific and Industrial Research Organisation), an Australian Government agency, with finding a way for computers to communicate with each other without wires. Remembering his research into black holes and the device he had made; O'Sullivan began to work on modifying it to work with computers. Because of the device's ability to search for a particular signal, even in an environment with tons of signals floating around, it was the perfect tool.

This modification led to the first-ever Wi-Fi and it earned CSIRO over $1 billion for the invention.

Without Wi-Fi, most of our modern-day devices would not work. Anything that is able to connect to the internet without a cable is dependent upon the creation of Wi-Fi. Most people wouldn't be able to go a week without it, so it's a good thing O'Sullivan was so determined to prove the existence of black holes.

He might not go down as someone who proved black holes exist, but modern-day life is completely indebted to him all the same.

MAUVE

Mauve is a pretty soft purple color that can sometimes border on being pink.

A fun fact about the color purple is that it was originally reserved exclusively for royalty because the dye was extremely expensive. It was also a very unique color that wasn't often seen and this helped set royals apart from the ordinary people.

Purple is a bright, fun color that you can find relatively easily today, but the story of the first purple or mauve dye is a rather interesting one. Not only was it entirely accidental, but it also became the first synthetic dye ever made and completely changed fashion.

Before synthetic dyes were invented, all dyes were made from natural materials. They were either extracted from insects—such as the cochineal, which is still used for red lipstick today—or taken from plants such as beetroot and other flowers. Purple came from an insect similar to a snail that was not only rare but also very difficult to extract the color from.

William Perkin discovered the first purple dye at only 18 years old, when he was trying to find an alternative to quinine, the medication used to treat and prevent malaria. In the 1850s, England was setting up military bases in many tropical countries where malaria was common. The problem was that quinine came from a particular tree, which only grew in South America and which was very expensive to process. Many scientists had tried to find a way to create artificial quinine, to make the medicine cheaper.

Perkin was working at his home in London, doing experiments on a compound called aniline, to see if he could get it to perform similarly to quinine; unfortunately, the experiment was a failure. He then tried to fix the failed experiment by adding alcohol and it was then that he noticed something strange. The alcohol was turning a purplish color.

Perkin may not have discovered something that made malaria medication cheaper, but he had discovered something that would revolutionize the world, especially fashion and design.

Synthetic dyes are cheap in comparison to natural dyes, and this discovery meant that purple was no longer reserved for the rich and powerful. It also launched a new era of trying to invent and find dyes for other colors. This exploded the world into a rainbow. Without Perkin's mistake, we would not have as bright a world as we do today.

THE TELEPHONE

Telephones are not as common today as they once were, even if cell phones are now replacing many of the old-school wired telephones.

However, once upon a time, telephones were a crazy thing that completely changed the world. Before telephones were as common as houses, people had to communicate through letters or telegraphs. Being able to get a response from someone instantly without having them in front of you was both strange and uncommon. Telephones really were life changing for many people.

Telegraphs came before telephones, and although they were also revolutionary, they were very simple in nature. You could send only one line of information at a time, to one point, and the lines had to be 'translated' to be understood on the other side.

Alexander Graham Bell, the telephone's inventor, was trying to improve the telegraph so that it could send multiple lines of information to multiple places at the same time. While he worked on this multiple-line telegram, but was also started to develop a "speaking telegraph," essentially the telephone before it was the telephone.

So, where does the accident come in?

At the time, Bell and his partner, Thomas Watson, did not know that sound signals could be sent electrically. Simply put, they had not yet realized that you could move sound through an electrical wire, which is what makes a telephone work. While he was working on the project, Bell accidentally plucked a wire that was attached to their prototype. This caused a vibration to travel through the system to the other end. After that moment, Bell and Watson began to focus all of their work on the telephone. They had moved sound through electrical wires. What they had been theorizing was now possible.

But this wasn't the only accident. The first test of the telephone was entirely accidental. While he was working, Bell accidentally spilled acid onto his pants. In his state of panic, he called out, "Mr. Watson, come here." To their amazement, Watson heard Bell on the receiver in the other room and came at once. They had gotten it to work, and the telephone was born.

The rest is history. The telephone swept across America and then the rest of the world. This invention changed how we understood electricity and allowed many more minds to come up with new and exciting things that we could do with just a simple wire.

DRY CLEANING

Dry cleaning always seems to be a special form of laundry that is reserved only for expensive work clothes. When I was younger, I used to think that they must use a special washing machine made from magic. Why else was it so mysterious and special?

Dry cleaning is nothing like washing clothes in a machine. For one, it is a process that uses oil as opposed to water to clean fabric. This method is meant to remove stains and preserve fabric in a way that water and soap never will.

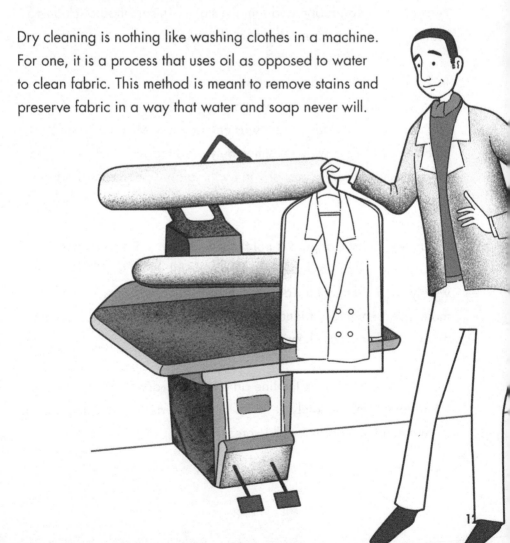

What seems even crazier to me is that dry cleaning has been around since the 1840s.

The story goes that a maid working in Jean-Baptiste Jolly's house knocked a kerosene lamp over onto a badly stained linen tablecloth, spilling lamp oil all over it. After inspecting the cloth, Jolly realized something; the linen appeared to be cleaner everywhere the oil had touched it. He had stumbled across a new way of cleaning fabrics.

Quickly wanting to capitalize on his discovery, Jolly set up the first-ever dry cleaning business that used gasoline-based products, such as kerosene to clean fabric and remove stains. This method of cleaning remained unchanged until the end of the 19th century.

In the 1900s, dry cleaners started experimenting with other chemicals, which could remove stains but preserve the color of clothes. The most popular one was chlorine, but Michael Faraday discovered "perc," which is still widely used today. The need to find other solutions was largely driven by the global petroleum shortages caused by the war.

Today, we know that perc is not the safest chemical and long-term exposure to it can be dangerous and harmful, but it is still the most widely used chemical for dry cleaning. Even though there are safer, more environmentally friendly options, most dry cleaners still opt for this more dangerous chemical.

From kerosene lamps to the fine art it is today, dry cleaning has come a long way. Unfortunately, it isn't a magical washing machine, but the story behind its origins is still interesting.

SUPERGLUE

Sticking your fingers together with superglue is both a terrifying and an exhilarating experience. Once the glue dries, you can't separate your fingers at all! And, you can quite easily remove the glue by washing your fingers under warm water, so they won't be stuck that way forever.

Superglue comes from World War II. Dr. Harry Wesley Coover, Jr., one of the inventors of the substance, was trying to create clear plastic gun sights for American soldiers. The problem was the compound he developed, cyanoacrylate, was far too sticky.

Imagine getting a gob of superglue in your eye—sounds like a disaster!

Coover and his team abandoned the substance at the time, and he did not go back to it until more than ten years later. Coover returned to his project when he was researching polymers (it's always polymers, isn't it?) and he then realized that the adhesive was unique. Unlike other adhesives, superglue could permanently stick two substances together without heat or pressure. This time around, Coover saw the potential of the substance and patented it as "Alcohol-Catalyzed Cyanoacrylate Adhesive Compositions/ Superglue" (O'Brien, 2021).

That's one long name. It was then repackaged as "superglue"—which is a lot catchier—and sold for commercial use.

Superglue was originally found during research for the military, and it actually evolved full circle. During the Vietnam War, doctors used the glue to close wounds as an alternative to stitches. This was much faster and allowed them to treat more patients in less time. It was also used as a quick fix to stop bleeding so medics had time to get patients to the hospital.

Superglue as it was then could cause skin irritation, but in 1998, a skin-safe version was developed and called "liquid bandages."

Superglue went from being too sticky to an adhesive we always knew we needed. It's not just good for household use, but has also been lifesaving in the medical sphere. Just try not to stick your fingers together next time you use it.

CONCLUSiON

So, there it is—50 inventions that all came from accidents. From food and medicine to toys and industrial items, we have journeyed through the many different inventions that came about from accidents and mistakes.

We often treat mistakes harshly and scold ourselves for making them. But don't shun your mistakes too quickly; as we now know, a large portion of the items in this book would never have been found if it weren't for mistakes.

Mistakes are a part of life. If we choose to learn from them, we can end up creating life-changing things, such as smart dust. When something goes wrong, it's best to look at the outcome with positivity and try to make the best of the situation. Who knows—you might just save the world.

They might seem like a lot, but in fact there are hundreds of other inventions that also arose from different intentions or little intention at all. That's part of the beauty of it all—it's so random and so difficult to control. Even ideas themselves can be fickle!

Getting curious about where things come from helped us discover the interesting stories of invention and accident. It also gave us a better understanding of how and why things work. Get curious about the world around you; from how the internet works to where chewing gum comes from. Curiosity is one of the most wonderful ways to make the world exciting and magical.

New things are being invented and accidentally discovered every day, and one day, your name might just end up in this book.

Made in United States
North Haven, CT
23 June 2023

38160095R00070